ROBIN SHARMA

DAILY INSPIRATION

from the Monk Who Sold His Ferrari

HARPERCOLLINS PUBLISHERS LTD

I dedicate this collection of quotes from the books in The
Monk Who Sold His Ferrari series to you, the Reader.
It takes a special person to have the courage to look within and
then do what needs to be done to create a life of authenticity,
abundance, happiness and wonder. So I honor you.

I also dedicate this book to my two children.
I am blessed to be their father.

January

Impact and Legacy

Personal Greatness

January 1

When I was growing up, my father, translating a Sanskrit saying, shared something with me that I will never forget. He said, "Son, when you were born, you cried while the world rejoiced. Live your life in such a way that when you die the world cries while you rejoice." We live in an age when we have forgotten what life is all about. We can easily put a person on the moon, yet we have trouble walking across the street to meet a new neighbor. We have technology to help us stay connected, yet in many ways we have never been less connected in the history of humankind. We know more than ever, yet we also know less, about what it means to be truly great—as a human being.

Impact and Legacy

January 2

Purpose is the most powerful motivator in the world. The secret of passion truly is purpose.

Impact and Legacy

January 3

Success cannot be pursued; success ensues. It flows as the unintended byproduct of efforts concentrated in the direction of a worthy cause.

January 4

The word *duty* is often viewed negatively in our culture. Many people don't like the idea of it, feeling that duty would restrict them and hinder them from living in the moment. To me, the word *duty* represents freedom and happiness. And leadership and authentic success is about doing what's right rather than what's easy.

January 5

Once you connect with some kind of higher purpose in your life, there will be a corresponding release of passion and energy. The secret of generating extraordinary levels of passion in your life is to discover your larger purpose. Once you find your calling, you get excited. And you begin to stand for something higher than yourself.

January 6

Look at people who discovered a cause that they gave their lives over to, people such as Benjamin Franklin, Mahatma Gandhi, Martin Luther King Jr., Mother Teresa, Albert Einstein and Nelson Mandela. They connected with some kind of a crusade that they decided their lives would represent. This engaged their hearts. This made them emotionally charged up about what they were doing. And once you can develop some emotional engagement around a pursuit, rather than simply an intellectual engagement, the excitement flows and the energy explodes.

January 7

Connect to a compelling cause with your heart, not your head. And then fasten your seatbelt because your life will soar. The mind can be a limiter. The emotions are the liberator.

January 8

You can find your cause—your crusade—exactly where you are. No one has to leave a job to find something to engage their heart and excite them. Often all that is required is that a person see things differently. And to take that first step. Today.

January 9

A cause to stand for unleashes energy, no matter if it's one about creating incredible experiences for the men and women who give you business or one that involves saving the world. All remarkable creations begin with energy—and commitment. Resolve to be extraordinary in all that you do.

January 10

Find your cause, and then do your work with pride and love—love is such an incredible force for good. It's the most powerful thing in the world.

January 11

In the past, most of us were content to have a job that simply paid the bills. But now, we crave so much more in our work. We want fulfillment, creative challenge, growth, joy and a sense that we are living for something more than ourselves. In a word, we seek meaning. One of the best ways to find the higher meaning in the work you do is to use the technique of creative questioning to become aware of the impact your work has on the world around you. Ask yourself questions like, Who ultimately benefits from the products and services my company offers? or What difference do my daily efforts make? Once you do so, you will start noticing the connection between the work you do and the lives you touch. This will inspire you.

January 12

One day, my father posted a poem by Rabindranath Tagore on the door of our fridge. It read simply, "Spring has passed, summer has gone and winter is here. And the song that I meant to sing remains unsung. I have spent my days stringing and unstringing my instrument." These words were about a man whose heart was filled with regret over a life half-lived. The time to start building your legacy is today, not ten years from today when you "have more time." Reflect on what it is you want to create in your life and, more importantly, what gift you wish to leave the world when you are no longer here. Greatness comes from beginning something that does not end with you.

January 13

Balance success with significance. What is the point of achieving great things without having a great impact? At the end of our lives, what will be most important is who we have become—and the difference we have made.

Impact and Legacy

January 14

One of the timeless truths of life can be stated simply: When you shift from a selfish compulsion to survive into a heartfelt commitment to serve, your life cannot help but explode into success.

January 15

The celebrated inventor Thomas Edison is well known for his statement "Genius is 1 percent inspiration and 99 percent perspiration." While I believe that hard work is essential to a life of real success and fulfillment, I think that being filled with a deep sense of inspiration and commitment to making a difference in the world is an even more important attribute.

January 16

One of the greatest lessons for a highly fulfilling life is to rise from a life spent chasing success to one dedicated to finding significance. And the best way to create significance is to ask yourself one simple question: "How may I serve?" All great leaders, thinkers and humanitarians have abandoned selfish lives for selfless lives and, in doing so, found all the happiness, abundance and satisfaction they desired. Joy comes from giving.

January 17

Each and every one of us needs to ask ourselves, not just as parents but as people, "What will my life stand for after I have died?" We need to think about the footprints we will leave and how future generations will know that we have lived. I'm not saying we all have to be Mahatma Gandhis or Mother Teresas. Those were the paths that were mapped out for those people—and that they chose to live. What I am saying is that we all need to conduct our lives in a way that will allow us to transcend ourselves.

January 18

All too often, people attempt to live their lives backwards: they spend their days striving to get the things that will make them happy rather than having the wisdom to realize that happiness is not a place you reach but a state you create. Happiness and a life of deep fulfillment come when you commit yourself, from the very core of your soul, to spending your highest human talents on a purpose that makes a difference in others' lives. When all the clutter is stripped away from your life, its true meaning will become clear: to live for something more than yourself. Stated simply, the purpose of life is a life of purpose.

January 19

Nothing so destroys the heart as the knowledge that you had the chance to manifest the gorgeous potential within you and you refused to accept the call.

January 20

We all have special talents that are just waiting to be engaged in a worthy pursuit. We all have some form of personal genius within us. We are all here for some unique purpose, some noble objective that will allow us to manifest our highest human potential while we, at the same time, add value to the lives around us. Finding your calling doesn't mean you must leave the job you now have. It simply means you need to bring more of your talents into your work and focus on the things you do best. Today, decide to be brilliant at what you do. And in how you live.

January 21

Success on the outside means nothing unless you also have success within. There is a huge difference between well-being and being well-off. The person with a rich inner life is the richest of all.

January 22

The most joyful, dynamic and contented people of this world are no different from you or me in terms of their makeup. We are all flesh and bones. We all come from the same universal source. However, the ones who do more than just exist, the ones who fan the flames of their human potential and truly savor the magical dance of life, do different things than those whose lives are ordinary. Foremost among the things that they do is adopt a positive paradigm about their world and all that is in it. Where others see adversity, they see opportunity.

January 23

People who feel superb about themselves generate superb results. Self-respect is a beautiful thing.

January 24

Your life is a treasure and you are so much more than you know. The life you live today doesn't have to be the life you lead tomorrow. Make a choice. Take a leap. Rise above your circumstances to your next level of greatness.

January 25

The mind is a wonderful servant but a terrible master. If you have become a negative thinker, this is because you have not cared for your mind and taken the time to train it to focus on the good. Remember, we become what we think about all day long.

January 26

The people who get on in life are those who dream big dreams and then take whatever risks are necessary to bring their vision to life. They face their fears directly, get into the game and live their days with courage. They break through their fear doors, no matter how scared they feel. It's better to be a lion for a day than a sheep all your life.

January 27

The best antidote for fear is knowledge.

Personal Greatness

January 28

Luck is nothing more than the remarkable marriage of relentless preparation with well-presented opportunity.

January 29

Most people spend the best years of their lives in the place of the known. They lack the courage to venture out into foreign territory and are frightened to leave the crowd. They want to fit in and are afraid to stand out. They dress like everyone else, think like everyone else and behave like everyone else, even if doing so doesn't feel right to them. They are reluctant to listen to the call of their hearts and try new things, refusing to leave that shore of safety. They do what everybody else does. In so doing, their once-shining souls begin to darken. Success lies in being true to yourself—and living life on your own terms.

January 30

Clinging to safe shores in your life is nothing more than making a choice to remain imprisoned by your fears. And it's impossible to discover new oceans without letting go of the shore.

January 31

Courage is not the absence of fear but the willingness to walk through your fear in pursuit of a goal that is important to you. You are among the living dead when you live in a safe harbor and cling to the known. You come back to life and your heart starts to beat again when you venture into the unknown and explore the foreign places of your life. The adventure and thrill of living returns. Remember, on the other side of your fears you will discover your fortune.

February

Personal Greatness

February 1

Saying that you don't have time to improve your thoughts and your life is like saying you don't have time to stop for gas because you are too busy driving. Eventually it will catch up with you.

February 2

Thoughts are vital, living things, little bundles of energy, if you will. Most people don't stop to consider the nature of their thoughts and yet the quality of your thinking determines the quality of your life. Your thoughts form your world. And what you focus on shapes your destiny.

February 3

You truly cannot afford the luxury of even one negative thought. A worrisome thought is like an embryo: it starts off small but grows and grows. Soon it takes on a life of its own. Stop feeding what doesn't serve you.

February 4

Awareness precedes change. Before you can change something in your life, you must first become aware of it and begin to really pay attention to it. You must build some awareness around it. You will never be able to eliminate a weakness you don't even know about.

February 5

The best possible use of your time, bar none, lies in cultivating your mind, heart, body and spirit so that you can bring more brilliance to this world. Awakening these four dimensions of your inner world is the best move you can make. Outer greatness is preceded by internal excellence. Your external life can never be larger than what exists within.

February 6

When you run inspiring, imaginative pictures through the movie screen of your mind, wonderful things start to happen in your life. Einstein said that "imagination is more important than knowledge." Spend some time every day, even if it is just a few minutes, in the practice of creative envisioning. All extraordinary acts begin with a dream.

February 7

So many of us have shifted our focus from a quest for the external to a voyage into the internal. For many, the human journey has become an inner journey. We have realized that the gateway to lasting success does not swing outward, it opens inward. The greatest treasures are the treasures that lie within. We, as a global community, are now beginning to think far more about the needs of our souls and devoting more time to activities like personal growth, being more loving and compassionate and leaving a legacy. Success is important but significance is even better.

February 8

Feelings are the doorways into your soul, and they must be acknowledged and then felt to completion. Feelings carry important information and serve to foster your self-relationship if explored fully.

February 9

As your awareness expands, you will become aware of things you previously could neither see nor understand. We don't know what we don't know—until we start looking within. All is good here. All that has unfolded for you is leading you to a fantastic place.

Personal Greatness

February 10

If you really want to improve your outer world, whether this means your career, your relationships or your finances, you must first improve your inner world. The most effective way to do this is through the practice of continuous self-improvement. Self-mastery is the DNA of life mastery. Greatness is an inside game.

February 11

In our society, we all too often label the ignorant as weak. However, those who express their lack of knowledge and then seek instruction find the path to wisdom before anyone else.

February 12

Zen tradition speaks of a beginner's mind: those who keep their minds open to new concepts—those whose cups are always empty—will always move to higher levels of achievement and fulfillment. Never be reluctant to ask even the most basic of questions.

February 13

Fear is a conditioned response, a life-draining habit that can easily consume your energy, creativity and spirit if you are not careful. When fear rears its ugly head, beat it down quickly. The best way to do that is to do the thing you fear. Fast.

Personal Greatness

February 14

Understand the anatomy of fear. It is your own creation. Most of the things we are afraid of never even happen. So why let your fears own your life?

February 15

All human progress, all of the advancements in the world—ranging from the discovery of fire to the creation of the personal computer—have come about by people who had the courage not to listen to the crowd but do what they felt was right, regardless of the fact it provoked uncertainty and fear within them.

February 16

To take risks is to provoke fear. But to take risks is to be most alive. We are most alive when we are taking risks, being bold and visiting the unknown spaces of our lives. Big risks, big life. Small risks, small life.

February 17

Why postpone your greatness? There will never be a perfect time to live your dreams and step into the poetic possibilities your life was meant to be. So why not take the leap today?

February 18

Every one of us creates a story about his own life, even if he only tells it to himself. For some, the story is all about being a victim. Playing the victim is easy. You do not have to assume any responsibility for the way your life looks. You can blame everyone else for what's not working in your life, never having to look at yourself and make the changes required. But when you play victim, you give away your power to that which you allege is victimizing you. It's a very impotent way to live.

February 19

Personal transformation is not a race. Actually, sometimes the harder you try to change, the longer it takes. So many people treat self-discovery like an extreme sport—rushing to get all their healing at a frenetic pace. They read book after book. They visit guide after guide and attend seminar after seminar. They want to know the answers to the big questions they are struggling with. But someone who cannot sit in the mystery of their lives and enjoy the process of personal growth is a person standing in fear.

February 20

You are what you think about all day long. You are also what you say to yourself all day long. If you say that you are old and tired, this mantra will be manifested in your external reality. If you say you are weak and lack enthusiasm, this too will be the nature of your world. But if you say that you are healthy, dynamic and fully alive, your life will be transformed. Words have remarkable power.

February 21

You will never be able to eliminate a weakness you don't even know about. The first step to eliminating a negative habit is to become aware of it. Once you develop an awareness about the behavior you are trying to change, you will be well on your way to replacing it with one that is more helpful. Just as shadows held into the light dissolve, weaknesses brought into the light of self-awareness begin to disappear.

February 22

Fear is the primary factor that causes people to live small, inauthentic lives. And most fears are illusions.

February 23

Freedom is like a house: you build it brick by brick. The first brick you should lay is willpower. This quality inspires you to do what is right in any given moment. It gives you the energy to act with courage. It gives you the control to live the life you have imagined rather than accepting the life that you have. Discipline is an antidote to regret.

February 24

The mind is a splendid tool, to be used for planning, patient reflection and learning from past mistakes so they will not be repeated. The mind will help you gain knowledge and receive education from life's teachings. But the mind must not run the show, as it does for most people. Balance living in the mind with operating from the heart. Actually, lead from the heart.

February 25

The mental chatter that fills most people's minds is mostly about why we shouldn't do something and the adverse consequences of failure. The mind all too often keeps us small.

February 26

One of the timeless truths of successful living can be stated simply: your thoughts form your world. What you focus on in your life grows, what you think about expands and what you dwell on determines your destiny. Life is a self-fulfilling prophecy—it gives you just about what you expect from it. Take a good, hard look at your environment. Your thoughts are shaped by the people you associate with, by the books you read, by the words you speak and by your daily physical surroundings. When you take steps to make the environment you work and live in a better one, you will quickly detect improvements in the way you think, feel and act.

February 27

To get the best from life, be completely present and mindful in every minute of every hour of every day. Yet, on most days, our minds are in ten different places at any one time. Rather than enjoying the walk to work, we wonder what the boss will say to us when we get to the office, or what we will have for lunch, or how our children will do at school that day. Our minds are like scampering puppies or, as they say in the East, like unchained monkeys, rushing from place to place without any pause for peace. By developing present-moment awareness and an abundance of mental focus, you will not only feel much calmer in your life, you will also unlock the fullness of your mind's potential. And that marks the beginning of greatness.

February 28

Without the ability to concentrate, a full and complete life is not possible. If you lack the mental focus to stay with one activity for any length of time, you will never be able to achieve your goals, build your dreams or enjoy life's dazzling process. Meditation is not some contrarian practice reserved for monks sitting atop mountains. No, meditation is an age-old technique that was developed by some of the world's wisest people to gain full control of the mind and, in doing so, to manifest its enormous potential for worthy pursuits. Meditation is a method to train your mind to function the way it was designed to function. And here's the key benefit: the peace and tranquility you will feel after twenty minutes of daily meditation will infuse every remaining minute of your day. You cannot afford not to discover the power of this 5,000-year-old mind-training discipline.

March

Personal Greatness

Destiny and Life's Purpose

March 1

Balance head with heart. Balance chasing dreams and making things happen with letting things happen and trusting in the higher plan. Balance an awareness that the purpose of life is to return to our greatest selves with an appreciation that we are human beings with various imperfections, who reside in a world with many lovely pleasures that can—and should—be savored without guilt.

March 2

When you go after what you want, with love and wild abandon, you tap into the energy that created the stars and the seas. A kind of magic begins to enter your life and things happen that defy your comprehension. Signs start to appear, suggesting that you are on the right track.

March 3

When you do your best and dedicate yourself to excellence, life supports you and puts wind beneath your wings. It sees a human being who is reaching for his ideals and trying to become what he was meant to be. That kind of effort never goes unnoticed by the eyes that watch over the world.

March 4

Every gift we have been given—and every one of us has gifts—has been given to us for a reason. With each of the gifts we have received comes the responsibility that we sculpt it and develop it and then apply it out in the world in a way that enriches the lives of other people.

March 5

People who are not willing to set an intention for all they want from life and then to boldly pursue it are ultimately people with much fear stirring within their hearts. Don't let your fears deny you your freedom.

March 6

To blame my moods, my inactions and my mistakes on the way the planets are aligned is to give away the power I have been given as a human being to the planets, the moons and the stars. It's a weak way to live. Remember, you are not your moods but a force far bigger than them. You are not your psychology but a power far wiser than it.

March 7

We are not our thoughts. Instead, we are the creators of the thoughts that flow through our minds and, given this fact, we can change our thoughts if we choose to do so. Just as you are not your thoughts, you are not your moods. You are the creator of the moods you experience, moods that you can change in a single instant. If you choose to do so, you can feel peace in a moment of stress, joy in a time of sadness and energy during a time of fatigue.

March 8

The way to an extraordinary life lies in exploring ourselves, in learning of our greatest capacities and in understanding who we fundamentally are as people. Then, equipped with this essential knowledge, we can go out into the world to do what we have been wired to do and create the goodness that we have been placed here to create. Remember, you have a duty to shine, and this world will be less of a place if you choose to play small with your life.

Personal Greatness

March 9

Self-examination is the first step to personal greatness.

Personal Greatness

March 10

Reflection is the mother of wisdom. Carve out some time each day to ask ourselves why we are here, how we are living and whether we are making the highest use of the gifts that life has given us. Make the time to think. Daily.

March 11

Most people believe that it takes months and years to transform their lives. Actually, you can literally change your life in an instant by making a single decision never to go back to the way you have been living—no matter what. What takes months, years and sometimes decades is the maintenance required to live by that decision.

March 12

Just as a shadow fades when brought into the sunlight, a fear invited into the light of our human awareness begins to evaporate. Look within. And resolve to build a better you.

March 13

What we resist will persist. And if we refuse to do the inner work required to look at and then work through our fears, they will always run us. But if we have the courage to self-explore and get to know our fears, they will move through us, and then be released. What we befriend, we transcend.

March 14

Make the time to confront your resistances and examine your-self when frustrations or fears surface, rather than making it about others and avoiding self-responsibility. That's a giant key to growing more powerful and peaceful as a person. Our lives are mirrors. And life sends us not what we want but who we are. As we shine more brightly and stand more greatly, our outer lives cannot help but follow.

March 15

No matter who you are and no matter what your background is, you still have the power to choose how you will process the events of your life. That capacity to choose the way we will interpret what happens to us is our highest human endowment. So don't expect others to change in order for your circumstances to get better. You go ahead and take the noble path. You make the changes that need to be made. Others around you will eventually follow. The best way to influence another is to lead by example. Become who you wish others would be.

March 16

Your beliefs in life are really nothing more than mental contracts you have made with yourself about the state of affairs you find yourself in. Some people believe they are too busy to hug their children many times a day to show them their love. In doing so, they have made a contract with themselves in an effort to justify that "fact." Some people believe that they can never live great lives because their pasts have been too difficult. In doing so, they have made a contract with themselves and resigned themselves to live by that "fact."

Personal Greatness

March 17

It is not what you are that is holding you back in life. It's what you think you're not. It is what is going on in your inner world that is preventing you from having all that you want in your outer world. And the moment you fully grasp this insight and set about ridding your mind of all its limiting thoughts, you will see almost immediate improvements in your personal circumstances.

March 18

Happiness does not arrive when you achieve certain things. It comes when you think certain thoughts and feel certain feelings. Happiness is nothing more than a state of mind that you create by the way that you process and interpret the events of your life.

March 19

There are four dimensions of your authentic self to awaken so you can become whole once again: your mind, your body, your heart and your spirit. When you awaken these four dimensions, you will remember who you truly are.

March 20

Reading the book of another person is a reflection of their truth. Hearing a speaker at a seminar means that you will hear their truth and their philosophy on the world and on life itself. That may be fine at this stage of your journey. Learning what others think will help you to figure out what you really think. But don't make the mistake of believing that the truth of another person is necessarily your own truth. True success arrives once you live by your philosophy. Trust yourself to lead you where you dream of being.

March 21

One of the natural laws that runs the world is that when you focus on what you don't want in your life, you actually block what you do want from entering. What you invest your attention in will grow in your life. Focus on what you don't want and you'll get more of it.

March 22

Feelings are like rainstorms, with a beginning, a middle and an end. If we stifle them, they will fester like wounds. If we pay attention to them and bring them into the light of our awareness, we will move through them and they will complete. And we will move to greater and greater health.

March 23

We always have choices as human beings. Each of us has far more choices than we are aware of. We think we are so limited in life that we have to live and do what we currently do. That's just more of the language that victims are prone to use. It's always up to you—how far along the path home from your social self to your authentic self you want to go. And when you assume personal responsibility for what's not working in your life and then bravely start taking action to improve what needs to improve, doors you didn't even know existed will begin to open up.

Personal Greatness

March 24

Patience is required on this path to truth and self-awakening. Your timing may not be life's timing.

Destiny and Life's Purpose

March 25

You are far greater than you have ever dreamed of being. And no matter what you are experiencing in your life right now, trust that all is good and unfolding in your best interests. It may not look pretty, but it is exactly what you need to learn for you to grow into the person you have been destined to become. Everything occurring in your life has been perfectly orchestrated to inspire your maximal evolution as a human being and bring you into your true power. Learn from life and allow it to take you where you are meant to go—it has your highest interests in mind.

March 26

The Abundance Principle holds that the more you give to others, the more you will ultimately receive yourself. I've discovered that if you want more abundance and prosperity in life, you need to give more. Abundance is an energy that circulates in the world, and the more you send out, the more you will see come back to you. Good things always happen to people who do good things.

March 27

Be patient and live with the knowledge that all you are searching for is certain to come if you prepare for it and expect it. Your answers are coming. Relax.

March 28

The mind craves external power, the kind based on worldly—rather than inner—things such as money, position and possessions. The problem with external power is that it is fleeting: when you lose the money, position and possessions, you lose the power. If you have tied your identity to those things, you will also lose a sense of who you are when they fall away. The only power worth anything is authentic power—that which comes from within.

March 29

The heart lives in the present moment, knowing that is where life is to be lived. The heart is concerned with healing into wholeness, love, compassion, understanding and service to other human beings. It is aware that each of us is connected at an unseen level, that we are all brothers and sisters of the same family and that happiness comes from giving and supporting the growth of others into their greatest selves.

March 30

Most of our evolution, as human beings, to date has been marked by a focus on the physical, on the external. It has, until now, all been about accumulation and hoarding. The dominant value has been "he who has the most wins"—he who has the most fame, he who has the biggest fortune, he who wields the most power over others. And given this value, "survival of the fittest" has become the name of the game. It's all about competition because we have come to believe that there is not enough for everyone to win. But this philosophy no longer serves us as a race. It is one born of scarcity. And behind this thought of scarcity is outright fear. Since our intentions and what we think create what we see in our outer world, all we see is lack—there's never enough for us. And so the cycle begins, we never feel as if we have enough and we are never happy.

March 31

From today onwards, take complete control of your life. Decide, once and for all, to be the master of your fate. Run your own race. Discover your calling and you will start to experience the ecstasy of an inspired life.

April

Destiny and Life's Purpose

April 1

As human beings, our tendency is to tell life to listen to what we want. But life doesn't work that way. It gives us what we need, what is best for us—what is in our highest interests. Your life will work much better once you begin to listen to life. Let it lead you rather than trying to push the river.

April 2

Trust that where life carries you is exactly where you are meant to be. Let go of all your resistance and move into a posture of surrendering to whatever is unfolding. Doing so is one of the ways you will ensure that you will walk the path of your destiny, your true path.

April 3

One of the greatest regrets people can ever have is getting to the end of their lives and realizing they did not fulfill their dreams. Getting to the end or even the middle of your life and waking up one day to the understanding that you did not dare, that you did not reach for the stars, that you did not realize even one-tenth of your potential will break your heart.

April 4

The past is a grave and it makes no sense to spend your life living in a grave. Every ending represents a new beginning. Or to put it another way, you cannot move forward in life if you're stuck looking in the rearview mirror.

Destiny and Life's Purpose

April 5

Most people don't discover what life is all about until just before they die. While we are young, we spend our days striving and keeping up with social expectations. We are so busy chasing life's big pleasures that we miss out on the little ones, like dancing barefoot in a park on a rainy day with our kids or planting a rose garden or watching the sun come up. We live in an age where we have conquered the highest of mountains but have yet to master our selves. We have taller buildings but shorter tempers, more possessions but less happiness, fuller minds but emptier lives. Do not wait until you are on your deathbed to realize the meaning of life and the precious role you have to play within it.

April 6

No one discovers their destiny. Your destiny will discover you—it will find you, provided you have done the preparation and inner work required to seize the opportunity when it presents itself.

April 7

Stop worrying about finding your destiny. Spend your time getting to know yourself. Tear down the façade you show to the world and do the deep inner work on yourself needed to know who you really are.

April 8

Most of us know what we need to do in order to live happier, healthier and more fulfilling lives. The real problem is that we don't do what we know. The mark of an exceptional character lies not in doing only what is fun to do or what is easy to do. The sign of deep moral authority appears in the individual who consistently does what he ought to do rather than what he feels like doing, showing a flawless execution of what's most important.

April 9

Trust that your timing is not necessarily nature's timing. Flow into the process. You are not meant to know all the answers, at least not right now. When you are ready for a piece of learning and a specific lesson, it will come. What fun would it be if you knew all the plot twists of a movie halfway into it?

April 10

Too many people can't handle the notion that their plans and goals will not unfold as they anticipate. That kind of thinking reflects a control issue on their part. And behind their need to control is often fear. Life has bigger plans for you than you can possibly know.

April 11

Yes, make plans and set goals. Work hard and go for what you desire. That's part of being a responsible person—it is true that setting intentions does make many of them come to life. But hold on to your plans and goals with a very loose grip. Often, the universe will send you a treasure in an unexpected package.

April 12

Unless you reduce your needs, you will never be fulfilled. You will always be like that gambler in Vegas, staying at the roulette wheel for "just one more spin" in the hope that your lucky number will come up. You will always want more than you have. Lifelong happiness does come through working and doing your part to realize your dreams. The key is not to make your happiness contingent on finding that elusive pot of gold at the end of the rainbow. The journey is always better than the end.

April 13

Within you lie the sun, the moon, the sky and all the wonders of this universe. The intelligence that created these wonders is the same force that created you. All things around you come from the same source. We are all one.

April 14

When you nourish your own mind and your own spirit, you are really feeding the Soul of Life. When you improve yourself, you are improving the lives of all those around you. And when you have the courage to advance confidently in the direction of your dreams, you begin to draw upon the power of the universe.

April 15

When you are ready to receive a certain lesson, you will receive the perfect experience or person who will represent an opportunity for you to learn that lesson. And once you get the lesson, time must elapse so you can integrate it. There's no hurry. It's all a beautiful journey. Trust that where you are, at any given point, is precisely where you are meant to be.

April 16

Let go of your need to control the path of your destiny. Because, no matter how hard you try, you just can't. Sure, you can make wise choices and your choices will have an impact. But ultimately, you are not in control. We are so arrogant as human beings. We think that we are more intelligent than the universe. This universe that created the sunsets and the rainbows. This universe that created the stars and the moon. We think that we know more about what's in our best interests than the source that created all that exists.

April 17

If you keep choosing to grow and walk in the direction of your fears, you will move to higher and higher stages of personal freedom and individual greatness. You will be able to discover what life's really all about. You will begin to know the universal truths and natural laws that govern the operation of the world. Once you know these, you can keep choosing to align yourself with them. And when you align yourself with the natural laws that run the world, your life automatically works.

April 18

Generally the things that we value most when we are in our twenties, thirties and forties become the things we value least at the end of our lives. And all those things that so many among us currently value least, like deep human connections, random acts of kindness, being in superb physical condition, devoting ourselves to excellence in our work, creating a legacy and carving out time each day to work on ourselves so that the best within us shines, will—in the end—reveal themselves to be most valuable.

April 19

On our deathbeds, none of us wishes we had more money in the bank or a bigger car sitting in the driveway. Instead, as we take our last few breaths, we wish that we had lived a life that was courageous, authentic and remarkably loving.

April 20

Each and every one of us has an incredible amount of choice in the way our lives ultimately unfold. It is by our specific choices that our ultimate destinies are created. It's almost as though a rough design or sketch of our lives has been made for us by that wise architect in the sky and it falls to us to draw out so many of the details.

April 21

There's no doubt that, as human beings, we cannot control all that happens to us—that's the fate part. Life runs along according to its own course. But what we do have enormous control over is the way we respond to what life sends our way. So that's the partnership: do your best—the very best that you know how to do in every dimension of your life—and then let life do the rest. It's really a delicate balance between making it happen and letting it happen.

April 22

We really can make our own luck a lot of the time, and good things generally do happen to people who do good things. But once you've done your absolute best, let go and trust that whatever comes is perfectly suited for the growth you need to evolve into your best self.

April 23

Many possible paths to our best lives have been written for us.

April 24

One of the most enduring of all the ancient laws of humanity is that we see the world not as it is, but as we are. By improving, refining and defining who we are, we see the world from the highest, clearest perspective. By mastering ourselves, we see the world and all its limitless opportunities and potential from the top of the mountain rather than from the bottom.

April 25

There are many paths to the mountaintop of peace.

April 26

Just as there are many routes you can take to get home from work, there are many routes you can take to get to your biggest life, the life that has been meant for you—and getting there is a homecoming of sorts as well. There are many jobs you can take that will get you to your destiny. Similarly, there are many soul mates available to you, each offering different lessons, but all able to help you grow into and awaken your best self. Getting home to the place of brilliance, love and fearlessness you have forgotten is the reason for your existence. Now, it's up to you which path you take as you attempt to get to your authentic life. Taking one path might mean a longer trip. Taking another might be like taking an expressway to your destination, with a smooth ride and cloudless blue skies. It's up to you. It is, in large part, determined by the choices you make within the moments of your days. You co-write the script that has been written for the story of your life.

April 27

Do good and be good. This world of ours is run according to a series of immutable natural laws, laws created by the same force of nature that built the world and sent you here. You cannot play a game like golf without knowing the rules. Well, life's like a game as well. And in order to play—and win—it's essential that you learn the rules. Live your life in alignment with them and your life will work.

April 28

Life wants you to win. Did you know that? You just need to get out of your own way and figure out the rules to the game as quickly as you can. And learning the rules of the game takes some effort, deep thinking in silent places and a genuine willingness to be a philosopher.

April 29

Everyone, if they hope to walk the path of their destinies to their biggest lives, must develop an appreciation for wisdom and a hunger to understand what their life is all about. This world would be a much better place if we all began to view ourselves as philosophers, thoughtfully—and artfully—being in the process of sculpting more delightful and meaningful lives.

April 30

Govern your daily actions by the timeless natural laws and you will automatically take the expressway to your greatest life. Disregard them and you'll be taking the long way home.

May

Destiny and Life's Purpose

Authenticity

May 1

Natural laws have governed the operation of the world since it began. They include core principles such as "always help others get what they want while you get what you want," "have impeccable integrity," "live in the present moment," "become the kindest person you know," "do your best and be excellent in all you do," "be true to yourself" and "dream bravely." Most of us know these principles but so few of us live by them.

May 2

While on his deathbed, Plato was asked by a friend to summarize his great life's work, *The Dialogues*. After much reflection, he replied in only two words: "Practice dying." The ancient thinkers had a saying that captured the point Plato made in other terms: "Death ought to be right there before the eyes of those who are young just as much as before the eyes of those who are very old. Every day, therefore, should be regulated as if it were the one that brings up the rear, the one that rounds out and completes our lives." Time is a priceless commodity and the best time to live a richer, wiser and more fulfilling life is now.

May 3

Life is not ignorant of your heart's longings. The part of the plan that has been written for you would never involve you doing something that was wrong for you. The whole idea is for you to be happy. Your destiny will never lead you to do something that would make you unhappy.

May 4

Remember that not everything will work out the way you want it to. There's a higher intelligence at play whose logic we often cannot understand. But if you just keep doing your best and letting life do the rest, accepting whatever comes with the knowledge that it's for your highest good, life will work out wonderfully. Better than expected, actually.

May 5

Human beings have been given free will for a reason: to take the steps required to bring our dreams and our destinies to life. There are lots of blanks we have the power to fill in and lots of dots to connect. You must put in the effort and make the sacrifices required to live the life of your dreams. Hard work, self-discipline and daily improvement are essential elements to becoming remarkable.

May 6

Every second you dwell on the past you steal from your future. Every minute you spend focusing on your problems you take away from finding your solutions. And thinking about all those things that you wish never happened to you is actually preventing all the things you want to happen from entering into your life.

May 7

After you've done your part by giving your best, relax and accept whatever comes back to you. You did all you could do. You acted responsibly and made the best moves and highest choices that were within your power to make. Now let the higher power take over and lead you to where you were meant to go. Let life take you to the path of your destiny.

May 8

Deep fulfillment in life does not come from accumulating objects but from actualizing our selves. Life isn't about collecting nice things, although there's nothing wrong with having them. But material pursuits shouldn't be the main purpose that drives your days. If it is, if you sacrifice time with your family and time developing yourself for time spent chasing objects, one day you will end up in a very sad state.

May 9

Confusion always gives rise to clarity over time and a moment does come when all the new learning becomes wonderfully integrated within your understanding. This is the beginning of real wisdom. Celebrate your confusion because it is simply a reflection of your growth. It is always a little chaotic when we leave the Safe Harbor of The Known and sail out in search of New Oceans.

Destiny and Life's Purpose

May 10

A wise sage met a beggar on the street one day. The beggar, not knowing to whom he was speaking, stopped the sage and asked him three questions: Why are you here? Where are you going? Is there an important reason that you are going there? The sage looked at the beggar and asked how much money he generally made on a given day. On hearing the honest answer given to him, the sage said, "Please come and work for me. I will pay you ten times that amount if only you will ask me these three questions before I do my meditation, early each and every morning."

May 11

We must frequently be in connection with our dreams. This universe of ours really is a friendly place and we would not be able to dream a dream without having the corresponding capacity to bring the dream to life. So keep making the time to think about your dreams and most closely cherished visions.

May 12

When a seeker on the path home to his true self—to his destiny—makes the decision to commit to walking toward the life that was meant for him, he will inevitably reach a point when he begins to see there is an entirely different world out there than he has ever known. This is an incredible place for a human being to arrive at. The limits vanish. He's ready to play with possibility.

May 13

As you leave the illusion that your life has been and start seeing the world for what it really is—a place of astonishing beauty—the pace of synchronicity in your life will quicken, as well. The more courage and conviction you show in living the life that the universe wants you to live, the more it will send you its blessings. It will give you its green lights.

May 14

Life is a growth school, ideally created to give us opportunities to learn each of the lessons we need to learn over the course of our lives on the planet. We live on "Schoolhouse Earth."

May 15

The past is water under the bridge and the future is a distant sun on the horizon of your imagination. The most important moment is now. Learn to live in it and savor it fully.

May 16

The saddest part of life lies not in the act of dying, but in failing to truly live while we are alive. Too many of us play small with our lives, never letting the fullness of our humanity see the light of day.

May 17

If you don't act on life, life has a habit of acting on you. And the days slip into weeks and the weeks into months and before you know it, your life will be over. Life's pretty short—no matter how long you get to live. Before you know it, you'll be dust. The point of wisdom is clear: stop living your life by default and start living your life by design. Get back into the game and take action to create the richer reality you know deep within your heart you were destined to create.

Destiny and Life's Purpose

May 18

The fact that you are asking big questions means you are grow-ing and awakening. You are leaving the crowd and becoming more conscious. Asking the right question is often how you find the right answer. In doing so you are discovering your truth and your authentic life.

May 19

Questioning unlocks the knowing that already exists within your heart. Ask the right question and I promise you, the answer you seek will surface—when the time is right. Questions are powerful.

May 20

One key natural law is this one: we never get more than we can handle. The path is lovingly planned for you and you will never receive more knowledge or truth than you are ready for. So all the pieces come to you only when you are ready to receive them. The student must be patient. Timing is important and the answers will come.

May 21

It is easy not to listen to what the Quakers call the "still, small voice within," that inner guide that is your personal source of wisdom. It is often difficult to march to your own drumbeat and listen to your instincts when the world around you pressures you to conform to its dictates. Yet, to find the fulfillment, abundance and outright greatness that you seek, you must listen to those hunches and feelings that come to you when you most need them.

May 22

You are on the path that has been walked by many great human beings before you. Your experience is not unique. Just keep the faith and continue choosing to go deeper and deeper within yourself. All of the answers that you are looking for are within you.

May 23

Life is a beautiful tapestry that has been perfectly woven together. We often do not receive what we want but we always receive what we need. We always get what's in our highest interest. That's one of life's greatest lessons.

May 24

No book could ever come close to teaching you what life itself can teach you if you live it with your eyes wide open and are awake to its lessons. To risk is to live. We play small, thinking that's a safe way to live when that's actually the most unsafe place to be. There is no safety in the Safe Harbor of The Known. That's just an illusion we get seduced by. And it can waste a good life.

May 25

A caterpillar cannot remain in the cocoon forever. A butterfly must emerge when the time is right. Just trust in nature's timing; it's not on the same clock as you. Remember that always. Your pain will pass—it always does.

May 26

There is a brilliant coherence that runs our lives. The more we can stop trying to force outcomes and simply be in the flow, the more the magic that our lives are meant to be will appear. Trying to make everything happen and force results without balancing things off with a willingness to let things happen is nothing more than control.

May 27

Not everyone who embarks on the path home will reach the destination. Most do not. But every single day offers us the opportunity to step a little closer to the ideal and become more of who we were meant to become. Every single day on the path brings greater blessings and more personal power—if we look for them. And the authentic power that you reclaim by working on yourself can never be taken from you. It stays with you for life.

May 28

Newborn children represent perfection and the state of being to which each of us is duty-bound to return. In the instant after you were born, you were fearless, pure love, innocent, infinitely wise, of boundless potential and beautifully connected with the unseen hand that created the universe. Most of us on the planet today have lost this connection to our authentic selves, this original state of being in which we were unafraid to walk toward possibility and reach for the stars. We have forgotten who we are.

May 29

Every single one of us has a light side as well as a dark side. Each of us has flaws to mend and wounds within us that cry out to be healed. Every single one of us has a splintered soul. This condition of imperfection is actually what makes us human.

May 30

You are a seeker, as are so many others on the planet today. The world is transforming as people who were once willing to live ordinary lives now step out of their comfort zones to explore the wilderness of the extraordinary. People are no longer willing to settle for being half-alive, divorced from their authentic power. They want to live greatly and soar among the clouds, to walk among the giants, to dance with the stars.

May 31

If you want to improve your life and live with all that you deserve, you must run your own race. It doesn't matter what other people say about you. What is important is what you say to yourself, being comfortable in your own skin. Be true to you. That's a key source of happiness.

June

Authenticity

Overcoming Adversity and Disappointment

June 1

Every human being needs to carve out the time to articulate a philosophy for his or her life—it's one of the most important things a person can do. Every person, to live truly and greatly, must define how he wants to live and what his biggest life will look like. We all need to have a statement on a piece of paper that we can revisit every morning while the rest of the world is asleep. Such a statement will serve as a moral compass to direct the choices of our day, and it will serve as an anchor to lock us into our best moves. Without a statement of philosophy, you will live your life by accident, reacting to whatever shows up within your days.

June 2

Most people spend more time planning their summer vacations than they do planning their lives. Be thoughtful about your life. Ask yourself: "How am I meant to live?" Question what you are meant to do, what things you will no longer tolerate in your life and what standards of excellence you will hold yourself to.

June 3

As infants, we really are perfect. We are still connected to the force that created the world. But as we begin to age, we adopt fears from the world around us. We want our parents to love and adore us. So we model them and take on their fears, limiting beliefs and false assumptions so we can be more like them. It's all done because we crave love. Who you are in this moment is not who you truly are. Rather, it's someone you've become as a result of being in this world. To clear all those fears that you have assumed from the world around you, you will need to go back and explore the source of all your fears. Then you'll have to work through them until they are no longer part of your psyche.

June 4

If you do not know who you are and what it is you truly want to be, then how can you recognize and seize your destiny when it presents itself to you? Know yourself and your destiny will find you. Clarity precedes mastery.

June 5

Truly successful people never seek to be like others. Rather, they seek to be superior to their former selves. Don't race against others. Race against yourself. Just resolve to be better than who you were yesterday and extraordinary things will unfold for you.

June 6

There's not a soul on the planet who doesn't have some fear that limits him from realizing his truest potential. The very condition of being human is one of imperfection and much of this imperfection arises due to the fears we have picked up as we have left the perfection of our original nature and traveled out into the world.

June 7

Stop bending to the demands of social pressure at the expense of your uniqueness. When you study the lives of the world's most successful and revered people, you will see that they did not care what other people thought of them. Rather than letting public opinion dictate their actions, they had the courage to let their hearts drive them. And in taking the road less traveled, they found success beyond their wildest dreams. Authentic success isn't a popularity contest.

June 8

It takes great strength to leave the crowd and be true to your original nature. But that's what leadership is all about—leaving the crowd and being true to who you really are. Running your own race. Living your truth.

June 9

We already are everything we've always dreamed of being. We've just forgotten it along the way. The main aim, then, is not to develop ourselves so that we become someone new. The endgame is really to discover who we truly are—and stand in all we are meant to become.

June 10

There's not one person on the planet who needs to improve—one cannot improve upon perfection and any suggestion that we need to do so only makes us feel more guilt about not being enough. The duty of every human being is not self-improvement but self-remembering. To self-remember is to reclaim the state of being and the authentic power that we lost when we left the ideal state of newborn children and walked out into this fear-filled world of ours, a world that spoiled us along the way.

June 11

Nothing's more important than having the bravery to live your life.

June 12

Most people who live among the crowd never press the pause button in their lives and stop for even sixty seconds to reflect on why they are here and what they are meant to do. Leadership and personal success require that we become more thoughtful than ordinary people. Stop being busy being busy. Become more reflective.

Authenticity

June 13

So as you continue along this path to your authentic life—as you leave the crowd and begin to live by your values, your beliefs and your heart's desires, you, as a seeker, will inevitably reach the "choicepoint." How you respond at this juncture will make all the difference in terms of how the rest of your life will unfold.

June 14

The purpose of life is all about making the journey home to wholeness, back to a place of integrity, back to your authentic self—the one that is fearless, all-knowing and of boundless love.

Authenticity

June 15

The process by which we leave our authentic self and become people that we are not—by taking on beliefs, values and behaviors from those around us—is known as enculturation. And as we leave our true selves, morphing into our social selves, a gap begins to form. We leave our original nature and assume the false mask of personality.

June 16

The greater the gap between who we truly are and the public personas that we present to the world, the less our lives will work. And the less joy we will experience. Why? Because there can be no happiness when we are betraying ourselves.

June 17

Darkness is nothing more than an absence of light: once you pour the light of human awareness and understanding into the darkest recesses of your being, you will become a being filled with light. Where there was once fear, there will be love. Remember what it means to be "en-light-ened": one filled with light.

Authenticity

June 18

With every move you make to be love when fear wants to own you, you reclaim—and remember—your original nature. Every single thing you do to present your biggest self to the world has the corresponding effect of helping you take back more of the authentic power that you were born with.

June 19

Most of us live our entire lives wearing a social mask that hides our true selves. Rather than showing the full colors of our humanity, we work hard to sculpt an image of the person we think the world wants us to be. We say the things other people want us to say and wear the clothes other people want us to wear and do the things other people want us to do. Rather than living the lives we have been destined to live, we end up living the lives of other people. And in so doing, we die a slow death.

June 20

Make the time to connect to your more playful side, the child within you. Take the time to study the positive qualities of children and model their ability to stay energized, imaginative and completely in the moment no matter what might be going on around them.

Authenticity

June 21

All of the great wisdom traditions of the world have arrived at the same conclusion: to reconnect with who you really are as a person and to come to know the glory that rests within you, you must find the time to be silent on a regular basis. Sure, you are busy. But as Thoreau said: "It is not enough to be busy; so are the ants. The question is what are you so busy about?"

June 22

As you move to higher and higher stages on the path to self-mastery, you will develop your own philosophy about the way life works and your place within it. You will select the truths of others that resonate with the deepest part of you. You will integrate the wisdom of others that rings true to you. And you will discard those ideas that do not speak to you and fail to make sense. In doing so, you will forge your own authentic code and personal constitution for living your biggest life. That's when you begin to shine.

Authenticity

June 23

When we awaken the spirit we nurture our highest self. This looks like different things to different people. To some, the spirit may involve prayer. For others, caring for the spirit may be reflected by communing with nature or listening to moving music. For yet others, awakening the spirit involves service, volunteerism, and living for a crusade larger than oneself.

Authenticity

June 24

Wise people remind themselves that every day could be their last. In doing so, they make it their commitment to be love rather than fear during the hours of their day. And they continually choose to be extraordinary—even when it's difficult—versus ordinary.

June 25

The more deeply we know ourselves, the more we can make authentic choices to make the leadership journey back home to the place that we have always known, at our core, we have wanted to be. In the Greco-Roman temples of the past, above the entrance one would often find the following words: "Know thyself and you will know the secrets of the universe and the gods."

June 26

Growth sometimes comes in difficult ways. But growth is always good. If you could look down at your life from a 50,000-foot perspective, you would see that everything that's happening is very beautiful. Priceless, actually.

Authenticity

June 27

We are literally afraid of who we truly are. We are afraid of our light. We are afraid of our brilliance. We are afraid of our highest possibility. We are afraid to stand tall and let our light shine into the world. With great gifts comes great responsibility. Most human beings don't want to look at their gifts because they don't want to deal with the responsibility that those gifts present—the responsibility to live fearlessly and make a difference in the world. And in doing so, they shrink from their greatness.

June 28

Conversation deepens conviction. The more you can converse about the things that you want to become, the more you will be able to dedicate yourself to doing what needs to be done. Words do have power.

June 29

Listening to the gentle whispers of the holiest places of the heart is all about discovering—and then heeding—the calls that come from the deepest place within you. Sometimes we hear these whispers when we are completely connected with nature, while we are out for a solitary walk in the woods on a magnificent autumn day, for example. Sometimes we hear these whispers while we are experiencing silence—in meditation or another form of contemplation. And sometimes these calls come to us in life's most trying and seemingly hopeless moments, like when someone we love dies or when one of our dreams shatters. The point of wisdom is simply this: pay attention and be aware of the inner voices that will lead you down the path of your destiny. Listen to what your heart tells you to do. And commit yourself to living out your destiny so you will leave a meaningful legacy.

June 30

Your wounds can be turned into your wisdom. Your stumbling blocks can become your stepping stones if you choose. Do not miss the remarkable opportunity that adversity and even tragedy presents. Your life can be made even better by the things that break your heart.

July

Overcoming Adversity and Disappointment

July 1

Immediately before a great victory, one will often experience a stunning defeat. The key is to maintain your focus and keep on believing. Don't give up.

July 2

No matter what happens to you in your life, you alone have the capacity to choose your response to it. When you form the habit of searching for the positive in every circumstance, your life will move into its highest dimensions. This is one of the greatest of all the natural laws of success and happiness.

July 3

There are no mistakes in life, only lessons. There is no such thing as a negative experience, only opportunities to grow, learn and advance along the road of self-mastery. From struggle comes strength. Even pain can be a wonderful teacher.

July 4

Suffering has always been a vehicle for deep spiritual growth. Those who have endured great suffering are generally the ones who evolve into great beings. Those who have been deeply hurt by life are generally the ones who can feel the pain of others in a heartbeat. Those who have endured adversity become humbled by life and, as a result, are more open, compassionate and real.

July 5

We may not like suffering when it visits us, but it serves us so very well: it cracks the shell that covers our hearts and empties us of the lies we have clung to about who we are, why we are here and how this remarkable world of ours really functions.

July 6

When we face hard times, we think the way we see the world reflects the way it really is. This is a false assumption. We are simply viewing the world from our hopeless frame of reference. We are seeing things through sad and hopeless eyes. The truth of the matter is that when we begin to feel better, our world will look better. And when we return to a state of joyfulness within, our outer world will reflect that feeling to us.

July 7

The world is a mirror. We receive from life not what we want but who we are. There are seasons to our lives and painful times never last. Trust that the winter of your sorrow will yield to the summer of your joy, just as the brilliant rays of the morning always follow the darkest part of the night.

July 8

Pain and adversity are powerful vehicles to promote personal growth. Nothing helps you learn, grow and evolve more quickly. Nothing offers you as big an opportunity to reclaim more of your authentic power as a person.

July 9

You would not have the wisdom and knowledge you now possess were it not for the setbacks you have faced, the mistakes you have made and the suffering you have endured. Once and for all, come to realize that pain is a teacher and failure is the highway to success. You cannot learn how to play the guitar without hitting a few wrong notes and you will never learn how to sail if you are not willing to tip the boat over a few times. Begin to see your troubles as blessings.

July 10

It is a truth that in our darkest times we are willing to go the deepest. When life is good, we live superficially; we are not very reflective. But when the seas get rough, we step out of ourselves and ponder why things have unfolded as they have. This leads to remarkable learning and growth. And life is all about growth and stepping into who we are meant to be.

July 11

We all travel different roads to our ultimate destinations. For some of us, the path is rockier than for others. But no one reaches the end without facing some form of adversity. So rather than fight it, why not accept it as the way of life? Why not detach yourself from the outcomes and simply experience every circumstance that enters your life to the fullest? Feel the pain and savor the happiness. If you have never visited the valleys, the view from the mountaintop is not as breathtaking.

July 12

Adversity tends to make us more philosophical. During times of challenge, we begin to ask ourselves the bigger questions of life, such as why does suffering happen, why do our best-laid plans not work out as we expect, and is life ruled by the silent hand of chance or the powerful fist of choice.

July 13

Things are never as bad as they seem. The situations that cause us sorrow are the same ones that introduce us to the strength, power and wisdom that we truly are.

July 14

There is nothing wrong with making mistakes. Mistakes are part of life and essential for growth. But there is something very wrong with making the same mistakes over and over again, day in and day out. This shows a complete lack of self-awareness, the very quality that separates humans from animals. Learn from your life and let your past serve you.

July 15

Once and for all stop being so hard on yourself. You are a human being and human beings have been designed to make mistakes. Coming to the realization that we all make mistakes and that they are essential to our growth and progress is liberating. We lose the need to be perfect and adopt a more sensible way of viewing our lives. We can begin to flow through life the way a mountain stream flows through a leafy forest, powerfully yet gracefully. We can finally be at peace with our true nature.

July 16

Failure is not having the courage to try, nothing more and nothing less. The only thing standing between most people and their dreams is the fear of failure. Yet failure is essential to success in any endeavor. It offers us lessons and guides us along the path of genuine success.

July 17

Some people learn from the errors others have made. They are the wise. Others feel that true learning comes only from personal experience. Such people endure needless pain and distress over the course of their lives.

July 18

The only people without problems and adversity are six feet under the ground. To live is to face problems, pain and suffering. These things are vehicles for growth, expansion and lifelong learning. They are part of the human experience.

July 19

Life's trials are nothing more than opportunities to collect wisdom and platforms to remember more of our authentic power, if we choose. But let's not forget, every life will have its share of triumphs and beautiful times as well.

July 20

No hardship ever lasts. No setback is forever. No misery lasts an eternity. It may seem as though adversity will never go away as we experience it but that's not the truth. Life has its seasons, its chapters, if you will. And the hard times are ultimately the times that sculpt us into something better.

July 21

We can reduce the suffering in our lives by assuming absolute personal responsibility for ourselves and making wise choices during the hours of our days. In this way, we do shape our destiny and have the power to live much happier lives.

July 22

Albert Camus once wrote, "In the midst of winter, I found there was within me an invincible summer." We really don't discover how powerful and resilient we are until we face some adversity that fills our minds with stress and our hearts with pain. Then we realize that we all have within us the courage and the capacity to handle even the greatest curves life may throw our way. Hard times do make us stronger.

July 23

Nothing that happens to us in life has any meaning other than the meaning we attach to it. Pain and suffering only come from judgment. As we release judgment and stop labeling things as "positive" or "negative" and simply accept them as opportunities to evolve into our biggest selves, our lives transform. And we become filled with peace and joy.

July 24

There really is no such thing as a "bad experience" or even a good one. Life just is. Just maybe, it's all good.

July 25

Suffering in life is really nothing more than the difference between the way things are and the way you imagine they should be. If you can come to accept the blessings of your present reality without always feeling that your life is hollow as compared to the lives of others, you will have taken a quantum leap toward becoming a happier, more peaceful person.

July 26

Before a seeker reaches the final destination of her biggest self, she will be presented with a trial. Before she reaches the treasure she has been longing for, she will be given a test. That's just the way life works on the path. If you study any great book of wisdom that describes this voyage of personal awakening, you will see that that seeker—or the hero—always faces some trial or adversity just before he gets the prize: the life that has been desired.

July 27

Most people give up just before they reach their dreams. Most people quit only steps away from getting everything they wanted. Don't let that happen to you.

July 28

Remember that life is a series of seasons. Every human being will have to endure the harshness of a few winters in order to get to the glory of the best summers. And never forget that winters do not last.

July 29

Keep in mind, at all times, that we grow the most from our greatest suffering. As we go through it, it hurts. But as we move through it, it also heals. When a jug of water falls to the floor and cracks, what was hidden within begins to pour out. When life sends you one if its curves, remember that it has come to help crack you open so that all the love, power and potential that have been slumbering within you can be poured into the world outside you. And, like a fractured bone, we do become stronger in the broken places.

July 30

During tough times, there is a tendency to let go of yourself. As you encounter adversity, have the discipline to maintain your routine. Get up early. Do your holy hour. Eat very well. Exercise. Spend time with nature and make sure that you do all you can to keep all four of your central dimensions—the mind, the body, the heart and the spirit—in fine operating order.

July 31

Feel your feelings. When you are facing hard times, some people will tell you to "just think positive thoughts." Such advice is not helpful. One must not rush to reframe a so-called negative event as a positive one. Doing so will throw you into denial. Feel through the feelings of hurt, anger or sadness that will naturally surface. It's okay to be with them. It's actually healthy to do so. Processing through them allows you to release them. Just don't get stuck in them. Grieve when you need to. Then, when it's time to go and move on, move on. Life is for the living.

August

Understanding Human Nature

Leadership

Honor and Strength of Character

Real Success

August 1

Only people in pain can do painful things. Only people who have been hurt can hurt others. Only people with closed hearts are able to act in less than loving ways.

August 2

To conquer, one first must yield. Rather than going against the change, one should flow with it. The nature of water is to flow. It goes with the current. It does not resist. It does not hesitate before it yields. But it is also one of the most powerful forces on the earth.

August 3

Keeping your cool in a moment of crisis can save you years of pain and anguish. A strategy to control your temper is what I call the "Three Gate Test." The ancient sages would only speak if the words they were about to utter passed three gates. At the first gate, they asked themselves, Are these words truthful? If so, the words could then pass on to the second gate. At the second gate, the sages asked, Are these words necessary? If so, they would pass on to the third gate, where they would ask, Are these words kind? If so, then only would the words leave their lips and be sent out into the world.

August 4

Leadership is really a philosophy for life. While CEOs and managers can be great leaders, so can caring teachers, committed scientists and compassionate mothers. Coaches lead sports teams and politicians lead communities. And it all begins within, by having the self-discipline to lead and know yourself. So Lead Without Title.

August 5

Visionary leaders show their people a higher, more inspiring reality when the rest of the world sees darkness. And they lead by example—ensuring their video is aligned with their audio.

August 6

True leadership of human beings lies in commending them rather than in condemning them. The deeper your relationship with others, the more effective your leadership of them will be. The best leaders are people who feel great about themselves.

August 7

To become an effective leader and a peak performer on the playing field of life, you cannot be a generalist, trying to be all things to all people. Specialists win. Focus your best talents on your biggest opportunities.

August 8

Every promise you break, no matter how small and seemingly inconsequential, steadily chips away at your character. Each time you don't honor a commitment, you chip away at the bonds between you and the people in your life.

August 9

Living life without a devotion to excellence dishonors the priceless gifts and talents that have been given to you.

August 10

Do the right things. Act in a way that is congruent with your true character. Act with integrity. Be guided by your heart. The rest will take care of itself.

August 11

No matter how big a house you have or how slick a car you drive, the only thing you can take with you at the end of your life is your conscience. Listen to your conscience. Let it guide you. It knows what is right. It will tell you that your calling in life is ultimately selfless service to others in some form or another.

August 12

Don't treat your words lightly. They are powerful and can have dramatic consequences. When you say anything, make certain you mean it. Say what you mean and mean what you say. Authentic communication is powerful. And rare.

August 13

Success lies in a masterful consistency around the fundamentals. The best get better by staying wildly focused on the simple principles of excellence, principles such as treating people well, working hard, refusing to give up, seeing opportunity where others see failure and staying true to you.

August 14

The secret of happiness is simple: find out what you truly love to do and then direct all of your energy toward doing it. Once you are concentrating your mental power and energy on a pursuit that you love, abundance flows into your life, and all your desires are fulfilled with ease and grace.

August 15

Lasting happiness comes from steadily working to accomplish your goals and advancing confidently in the direction of your life's purpose. This is the secret to kindling the inner fire that lurks within you.

August 16

The happiness you are searching for comes through reflecting on the worthy aims you are dedicated to achieving and then taking action daily to advance them. This is a direct application of the timeless philosophy that prescribes that those things that are most important should never be sacrificed to those things that are the least important.

August 17

Have your beautiful things but do not be imprisoned by them. Own them but do not let them own you. Give the main aim of your life over to far more important pursuits such as discovery of your highest potential, giving of yourself to others and making a difference by living for something more important than yourself. Success is fine but significance is the real name of the game.

August 18

What's the point of spending your life climbing a mountain, only to discover you've scaled the wrong one?

August 19

Remember that there are many forms of wealth, financial wealth being only one of them. One who has rich relationships and a loving community around her is, in my mind, wealthy. One who has a life of excellent health, adventure, excitement and continuous learning has wealth of a different sort. And one who is deeply connected to all of life and wakes up every morning feeling deeply at peace and aware of the truth must certainly be considered to be one who has accumulated yet another form of riches. The crowd—our tribe called Society—has taught us that economic wealth is the only type of wealth we should chase. Not true.

August 20

Money is only a byproduct of adding value and doing good for others. Focus on being great at what you do. Dedicate yourself to offering others all you can to make their lives better. Be truly outstanding in every element of your professional and your personal life. Create extraordinary value for others. The money will follow.

August 21

All too often we get caught up in thinking that we need to achieve certain heroic acts in order to validate our lives and bring us great success. We get fooled into believing we must accumulate expensive toys and an excess of belongings in order to be fulfilled at the end of the day. But that's not the way to real happiness. Real and lasting happiness comes through the progressive accumulation of unforgettable memories and special moments.

August 22

Living an excellent life is a manifestation of self-love. Someone who conducts his life as if he were one of the greatest people on the planet—a true heavyweight—is someone who not only has enormous self-respect but one who has deep respect for the force of nature that created him.

August 23

A seeker on the path home to his or her authentic and biggest self will always have to face fears he or she never knew existed. While living an unconscious life, many of our fears live within the realm of our subconscious minds. Consciously, we do not even know they are there. They lie dormant within us. But they are, affecting every one of our choices and running our lives at an invisible level. As we awaken and choose to see our lives from a more truthful frame of reference, our fears begin to see the light of day—and we must confront them if we want to transcend them.

August 24

Create a life that will be considered a work of art. You have that potential. We all do, as a matter of fact. It all comes down to whether you want to do the inner work required to get there. Self-mastery is where life mastery begins. Your outer world cannot be bigger than you.

August 25

Writing in a journal on a regular basis is very powerful. This helps you get to know yourself and deepen your self-relationship. Your journal should be a place you visit and examine yourself. With the awareness that brings, you can then pledge to make better choices. And better choices lead to better results.

August 26

If you have the courage to respect your body—the temple that houses the person that you are—personal mastery will not be far away. Each time you get into the gym for a workout on a day you just don't feel like exercising, you grow a little stronger as a human being. Each time you go out for a run on a cold winter's day when under the covers feels like the best place to be, you actualize your humanity just a little more. Working on improving your physical condition is a great way to improve your character and enrich the quality of your life. Good health is true wealth. What's the point of being the richest person in the graveyard?

August 27

In life, the little things are actually the big things. And the quality of success you will experience in your life ultimately depends upon the tiny choices you make every minute of every hour of every day.

August 28

One of the timeless secrets to a long, happy life is to love your work. The golden thread running through the lives of history's most satisfied people is that they all loved what they did for a living. When psychologist Vera John-Steiner interviewed one hundred creative people, she found they all had one thing in common: an intense passion for their work. Spending your days doing work that you find rewarding, intellectually challenging and fun will do more than all the spa vacations in the world to keep your spirits high and your heart engaged.

August 29

One of the most powerful things you can do is to write the story of your life in advance. It may not turn out exactly as you articulate it, but as the old saying goes: "If you don't know where you're going, any road will get you there." Better to have a plan in place than no plan at all. Planning is a powerful act of personal responsibility.

August 30

Happiness is not about chasing greater net worth—it's about cultivating a greater self-worth. It's not about having more money but about finding more meaning. And it's not about only being successful but about being truly significant—a person who creates lasting value in the world.

August 31

Maturity as a human being is loving what you have rather than worrying too much about having what you love.

September

Extraordinary Achievement

September 1

Failure is a choice. Nothing can stop a man or a woman who simply refuses to be kept down. Just make a decision from the center of your heart that, no matter what happens to you, you will keep walking the authentic path and consistently stay true to crafting a remarkable life.

September 2

The Law of Diminishing Intent says that the longer you wait to implement a new idea or strategy, the less enthusiasm you will have for it. Act daily on your strategy for change before it dies a quick death, burying your future vision with it. World-class people never leave the site of a great idea without taking some action to bring it to life. Ideation without execution is nothing more than delusion.

September 3

Most ineffectiveness stems from the fact that most people do not have the self discipline to do what they know they should do when they have to do it. They put off doing the important things in business and in life in favor of the easy and immediate things. But then they get to the end and realize that they lost a life.

Extraordinary Achievement

September 4

Doing the same things every day will not deliver new results. To change the results you are getting, you must change the things you are doing.

September 5

The real secret of personal effectiveness is concentration of purpose. There are activities that are worthy of your energy and attention and there are activities that are unworthy of them. The real secret of getting things done is knowing what things need to remain undone. Focus is central to success. As Confucius observed, "The person who chases two rabbits catches neither."

September 6

Never forget the importance of each and every one of your days. Your days are your life in miniature. As you live your days, so you live your life. Don't waste even a single one of them. The past is history and the future is just a figment. This day, the present, is really all you have. But what you do today powerfully influences what tomorrow will look like.

September 7

Quick fixes do not work. All lasting inner change requires time and effort. Persistence is the mother of personal change. And great things don't happen without hard work and sacrifice.

Extraordinary Achievement

September 8

Calculated risk taking will pay huge dividends. How will you ever get to third base with one foot on second? The biggest risk is not taking risks.

September 9

The things that get committed to paper are the things that are committed to in life. And the things that get scheduled are the things that get done.

September 10

The more disciplined you are with yourself, the easier life will be on you. The stricter you are with yourself, the gentler life will be on you. When you get stronger with yourself and rein in all those weaker impulses and have the self-discipline to do what's right—every time—your life is certain to turn out great.

September 11

One would think that the more we relax and have fun the more we will have the chance to experience true happiness. However, a key source of happiness can be stated in a word: achievement. Success is really about the progressive achievement of outcomes that are important to you. And creating the lives we want always brings the feeling of satisfaction and joy. The point is to have fun—while you achieve great things.

September 12

You will never be able to hit a target that you cannot see. People spend their whole lives dreaming of becoming happier, living with more vitality and having an abundance of passion. Yet they do not see the importance of taking even ten minutes a month to write out their goals and to think deeply about the meaning of their lives. Goal-setting will make your life magnificent. Your world will become richer, more delightful and more spectacular. Remember, clarity precedes mastery.

September 13

Pressure is not always a bad thing. Pressure can inspire you to achieve great ends. People often achieve magnificent things when their backs are up against the wall and they are forced to tap into the wellspring of human potential that lies within them.

September 14

A burning sense of passion is the most potent fuel for your dreams.

September 15

Courage allows you to run your own race. Courage allows you to do whatever you want to do because you know that it is right. Courage gives you the self-control to persist where others have failed. Ultimately, the degree of courage you live with determines the amount of fulfillment you receive.

September 16

The only limits on your life are those that you set yourself. When you dare to get out of your circle of comfort and explore the unknown, you start to liberate your true human potential.

September 17

Get into the arena, forget about the critics and play big with the gifts of your days. If you listen to your critics, you will never do anything great with your life. Life is short and the years will slip away very quickly, like grains of sand passing through your fingers on a hot day at the beach. You were meant to shine and let your talents see the light of day.

September 18

In order to awaken your best life, it's important that you "die while you are alive." Most people live as if they have all the time in the world. They wish they had more time in their days and yet they waste the time they have. They put off living until some event in the future occurs. In order to awaken to your best life, every day should be lived as if it were your last day on the planet.

September 19

What sets highly actualized people apart from those who never live inspired lives is that they do those things that less developed people don't like doing—even though they might not like doing them either.

September 20

Truly successful people, those who experience deep happiness daily, are prepared to put off short-term pleasure for the sake of long-term fulfillment.

September 21

There is but one failure in life and that is the failure to try. The greatest failure in life is the unwillingness to play your highest game and walk toward the places that frighten you.

September 22

Before Columbus, all previous adventurers sailed close to the shore, within sight of land. That was the accepted way to sail. Columbus dared to be different. He refused to do what all others had done. He took a risk: he sailed perpendicular to the shore—straight out to sea. And because he let go of the known and had the bravery to sail out into the unknown, he became one of our greatest heroes.

Extraordinary Achievement

September 23

All progress comes from unreasonable people, people who follow their hearts and the instructions of their consciences rather than the commands of the crowd. All progress has come from risk-takers and men and women who were willing to visit the places that scared them. Greatness arrives once you refuse to buy into what others see as impossible.

September 24

Knowledge is only potential power. For the power to be manifested, it must be applied. Most people know what they should do in any given situation, or in their lives, for that matter. The problem is that they don't take daily, consistent action to apply the knowledge and realize their dreams.

September 25

If you want to live greatly, you must also be willing to risk greatly. To get to the pearls, the diver needs to be willing to go deep and visit the places that the timid souls would never visit.

September 26

You will always feel a little discomfort when you are install-
ing a new habit. It's sort of like breaking in a new pair of
shoes—at first it's a little hard to wear them but soon they
fit like a glove. The best amongst us get comfortable being
uncomfortable.

September 27

Remarkable people are priority-driven. This is the secret of time mastery. Build your days around your priorities and you will play in rare air.

September 28

The real value of setting and achieving goals lies not in the rewards you receive but in the person you become as a result of reaching your goals and arriving at your mountaintop. When you achieve a goal, whether that goal was to be an extraordinary leader or a better parent, you will have grown as a person in the process. Often, you will not be able to detect this growth, but the growth will have occurred at an invisible level. You have built awareness and self-discipline, discovered new things about your abilities and manifested more of your human potential. These are rewards in and of themselves.

September 29

Most of us live as if we have an infinite amount of time to do all the things we know we must do to live a full and rewarding life. And so we procrastinate and put the achievement of our dreams on hold while we tend to those daily emergencies that fill up our days. This is a certain recipe for a life of regret. Commit yourself to managing your time more effectively. Develop a keen sense of awareness about how important your time really is. Don't let people waste this most precious of commodities, and invest it only in those activities that truly count.

September 30

The more you ask, the more you get, but it takes practice to get good at it. Success is a numbers game. As the Buddhist sages observed, "Every arrow that hits the bull's eye is the result of one hundred misses." Flex your "asking muscles" by asking for a better table at your favorite restaurant, for a free second scoop at your local ice cream shop or for a complimentary upgrade on your next airline flight. You might be surprised at the abundance that will flow into your life when you just ask sincerely for the things you want.

October

Extraordinary Achievement

Best Practices

October 1

To build a will of iron, it is essential to take small, tiny acts in tribute to the virtue of personal discipline. Routinely performed, the little acts pile one on top of another to eventually produce an abundance of inner strength. Perhaps the old African proverb says it best: "When spider webs unite, they tie up a lion."

October 2

You need not change your world in a day. Start off small. The thousand-mile journey begins by taking that first step. We grow great by degrees. Small daily steps lead to stunning results over time.

October 3

Those who use time wisely from an early age are rewarded with rich, productive and satisfying lives. Those who have never been exposed to the principle that "time mastery is life mastery" will never realize their enormous human potential. And they will live a life full of regret.

October 4

Plan your week and manage your time creatively. Have the discipline to focus your time around your priorities. Shift to lean. Move from complexity to simplicity. The most meaningful things in your life should never be sacrificed to those that are the least meaningful. And remember, failing to plan truly is planning to fail.

October 5

Never forget that time spent enriching your non-work hours is never a waste. It makes you tremendously efficient during your working hours. Our biggest ideas often come during our most relaxed times.

October 6

When you devote yourself to excellence in everything you do, you begin to feel a greater sense of positive pride about the way you are conducting your days. This in turn increases self-respect and confidence, which, in turn, release greater energy and passion. You begin to feel good about yourself. People who feel good about themselves do great work and create remarkable things. And this, in turn, just makes them raise their standards of excellence even higher. It's an upward spiral that takes people to ever-increasing places of joy, meaning and internal peace.

October 7

Make being extraordinary your way of being—your default.

October 8

Remember that when you settle for mediocrity in the small things, you will also begin to settle for mediocrity in the big things. And anything less than a conscious commitment to extraordinary personal performance is an unconscious commitment to ordinary personal performance.

October 9

A golden thread of a highly successful and meaningful life is self-discipline. Discipline allows you to do all those things you know in your heart you should do but never feel like doing.

October 10

Without self-discipline, you will not set clear goals, manage your time effectively, treat people well, persist through the tough times, care for your health or think positive thoughts.

October 11

Protect your time. Learn to say no. Having the courage to say no to the little things in life will give you the power to say yes to the big things.

October 12

Encourage yourself to do more and to experience more. Harness your energy to start expanding your dreams. Yes, expand your dreams. Don't accept a life of mediocrity when you hold such infinite potential within the fortress of your mind. Dare to tap into your greatness. This is your birthright.

October 13

Act as if failure is impossible, and your success will be assured. Wipe out every thought of not achieving your objectives, whether they are material or spiritual.

October 14

Be brave, and set no limits on the workings of your imagination. Never be a prisoner of your past. Become the architect of your future.

October 15

There is a difference between simply existing and truly living. There is a distinction between simply surviving and really thriving. The sad thing is that most people have lost sight of the human gifts that lie within them and have resigned themselves to spending the best years of their lives watching television in a subdivision. Too many people spend more time focusing on their weaknesses than developing their strengths. By concentrating on what they don't have, they neglect the talents they do have. The greatest people who have gone before us all had a simple strategy that ensured their success: they knew themselves. They made the time to reflect on their core abilities—those special qualities that made them unique—and spent the rest of their lives refining and expanding them.

October 16

When you set big goals and chase big dreams, you are engaging in a hugely creative act. You are using your imagination and your abilities to build something wonderful. That's creativity in action.

Extraordinary Achievement

October 17

Staying in your room and meditating or praying all day for the life of your dreams is not going to give you the life of your dreams, and believing differently is nothing more than engaging in magical thinking. The best among us are people of action. Personal leadership is all about getting important things done. Results matter.

October 18

Chase your dreams. Do all you can to build the life you want. Visit the places that scare you and do not shrink from the greatness that you know in your heart you were meant to present to the world. And once you've done everything in your power, as a human being, to make your desires happen—and only then—let go of outcomes.

October 19

It is easy to say yes to every request on your time when the priorities of your life are unclear. When your days are not guided by a rich and inspiring vision for your future, a clear image of an end result that will help you act more intentionally, it is not hard for the agendas of those around you to dictate your actions. The solution is to be clear about your life's highest objectives and then to learn to say no with grace.

October 20

Happiness is our birthright. We have been hardwired to do extraordinary things with our lives and present exceptional gifts to the world.

October 21

All of the geniuses who have graced this planet before us had one thing in common—they concentrated their lives on cultivating the gifts that made them special. Take Einstein, for example. He had the good sense to figure out that he had a remarkable aptitude for physics, and then spent the rest of his life refining that gift. He did not move into the fields of biology or chemistry. He specialized in his core competency. And because he stayed with what he did best and dedicated years and years to this mastery, a point eventually came when he achieved greatness as a human being.

October 22

Having clearly defined goals offers so many benefits. First, setting goals restores a sense of focus in our lives, lives that have become complicated by too many options. In this age we live in, there are simply far too many things to do at any given time. There are many distractions competing for our attention. Goals clarify our desires and help us to focus on only those activities that will lead us to where we want to go.

October 23

Become a person of action, one of those indomitable souls who goes out and hunts down his greatest life. Do the best that you know how to do. And then let go and accept whatever comes to you with a happy heart and perfect certainty that this is what nature intended for you.

October 24

It takes great resolve and power to leave the gravitational forces of the crowd and begin to live more truly. The space shuttle uses more fuel during its first three minutes after take-off than it requires during the remainder of its orbit around the entire earth for this same reason: there is a pull exerted by the world that takes great energy to overcome. But overcome it you must, to avoid a life of regret and sadness.

October 25

Every act of courage, every act of goodness and every act of self-responsibility will have an immediate payoff for you: each time you act with love rather than fear, you become more of who you were meant to be. Every time you reach for your dreams and listen to your heart, you remember a little bit more of who you are. And you gently transform.

October 26

When Olympic athletes return home from the games, some of them suffer from what psychologists call POD (Post-Olympic Depression). It seems that having achieved the pinnacle of success, there is no higher target for them to aim for and so life loses its meaning. To maintain a healthy level of optimism and passion for life, you must keep on setting higher and higher goals. On attaining one goal, whether it is a career goal or a personal one, it is essential that you quickly set the next one. Make certain your goals are worthy of you. Make sure they are the kind of challenges that will force you to reach into your heart and bring out the best within you, helping you grow in the process.

October 27

One of the most wonderful things about time is the fact that you cannot waste it in advance. No matter how much time you have squandered in the past, the next hour that comes your way will be perfect, unspoiled and ready for you to make the very best of it. If you so choose, tomorrow can be the day that you start getting up earlier, reading more, exercising, eating well, worrying less and playing at a level called extraordinary. No one is stopping you from opening your journal and, on a blank page, rewriting the story of your life. This very minute, you can decide the way you would like it to unfold, change the central characters and create a new ending. The only question is will you choose to do so?

October 28

If you do not act on life, life will act on you. The days will slip into weeks and the weeks into months . . . before you know it, your life will be over. Do not let the brilliant and beautiful treasure of your life slip away.

October 29

It's always darkest before dawn. A time comes in everyone's life when they have to play at the edges and take some big chances. A time comes for every seeker when he or she knows, deep down in the heart, that refusing to take the risk will resign him or her to a life of mediocrity. But making the leap, though it involves great fear along with great courage, will allow them to travel to a whole new land. A land of potential, happiness and freedom. Go deep and listen to the inner voice within you. Then trust in its guidance.

October 30

Never ever give up when a trial presents itself on the path. And many trials will present themselves along the way. Yes, before your greatest victory you will certainly face your greatest challenge. With an awareness that this is all part of the route that you must travel to return home to your authentic self, it will be easier for you: you will be prepared.

October 31

Join the Hope Club. Big, beautiful and seemingly impossible goals are superb vehicles to keep you inspired as you walk through adversity. When you are reaching for great and noble goals that speak to the best within you, your desire to reach them will pull you through the tough times that you will encounter along the seeker's path.

November

Best Practices

Building Remarkable Relationships

November 1

Getting up early is a gift you give to yourself. Few disciplines have the power to transform your life as does the habit of early rising. There is something very special about the first few hours of the morning. Time seems to slow down and a deep sense of peace fills the air. Joining the Five o'Clock Club will allow you to start controlling your day rather than letting your day control you. Winning the "Battle of the Bed" and putting "mind over mattress" by rising early will provide you with at least one quiet hour for yourself during the most crucial part of your day: the beginning. If spent wisely, the rest of your day will unfold in a wonderful way.

November 2

According to one study, the average four-year-old laughs three hundred times a day while the average adult laughs about fifteen times a day. With all the obligations, stresses and activities that fill our days, we have forgotten how to laugh. Daily laughter has been shown to elevate our moods, promote creativity and give us more energy. Comedian Steve Martin reportedly laughs for five minutes in front of the mirror every morning to get his creative juices flowing and to start his day on a high note.

November 3

Natural surroundings serve to stifle the endless chatter that fills our minds so that our true brilliance can be liberated. While you spend time enjoying nature, observe your surroundings with deep concentration. Study the complexity of a flower or the way the current moves in a sparkling stream. Take your shoes off and feel the grass under your feet. Give silent thanks that you have the privilege of enjoying these special gifts of nature. Life's simplest pleasures are life's best ones.

November 4

You become your environment. Become more selective in the news you expose your mind to. Be more deliberate in the way you read your newspaper and in the way you watch your television. Before you start reading the morning paper, have a purpose in mind. Use it as an information tool to serve you and to make you wiser rather than as an excuse to help you pass time. And resolve to expose yourself to influences that help you become the person you want to be.

November 5

It takes about 21 days to develop a new habit. Yet most people give up on creating a positive life change after only the first few days when they experience the stress and pain that is always associated with replacing old behaviors with new ones. Once you get past those first 21 days you will find that staying on course with a new habit will be far easier than you imagined. Take the time to study your personal habits and promise to make the necessary changes. The quality of your life will be determined in large measure by the nature of your habits.

November 6

Spending one hour a day working on yourself will surely give you dramatic results in thirty days—provided you do the right things. It takes about one month to fully install a new habit. After this period, the behaviors, strategies and tools you are embracing will fit like a second skin. The key is to keep on practicing them every day if you want to keep on seeing the results. Commitment is a powerful thing.

November 7

As you prepare your body, so you prepare your mind. As you train your body, so you train your mind. Take some time every single day to nourish the temple of your body through vigorous exercise. Get your blood circulating and your body moving. There are 168 hours in a week. At least five of those hours should be invested in some form of physical activity. Health is something most of us take for granted until we lose it. Don't let that happen to you.

November 8

Develop a lust for learning. Read regularly. Reading for 30 minutes a day will do wonders for you. Do not read just anything. Be very selective about what you put into the garden of your mind. It must be immensely nourishing. Make it something that will improve both you and the quality of your life. Something that will inspire and elevate you.

November 9

According to *U.S. News & World Report*, over the course of your lifetime, you will spend eight months opening junk mail, two years unsuccessfully returning phone calls and five years standing in line. Given this startling fact, one of the simplest yet smartest time management strategies you can follow is to never go anywhere without a book under your arm. While others waiting in line are complaining, you will be growing and feeding your mind a rich diet of ideas found in great books.

November 10

Solitude and quiet connect you to your creative source and release the limitless intelligence of Life.

November 11

Make the time to think. Get into the regular habit of introspection. By looking at what you are doing, how you are spending your day and the thoughts you are thinking, you give yourself a benchmark for measuring improvement. The only way to improve tomorrow is to know what you did wrong today.

November 12

To let go of the mental clutter that your problems tend to generate, list all your worries on a piece of paper. If you do so, they will no longer be able to fester in your mind and drain your valuable energy. This simple exercise will also permit you to put your problems into perspective and tackle them in an orderly, well-planned sequence. It will help you move to freedom and let go of the past.

November 13

The 10-minute period before you sleep and the 10-minute period after you wake up profoundly influence your subconscious mind. Only the most inspiring and serene thoughts should be allowed into your mind at those times.

November 14

Remember that it is the quality and not the quantity of sleep that is important. It is better to have six hours of uninterrupted deep sleep than even ten hours of disturbed sleep. The whole idea is to provide your body with rest so that its natural processes can repair and restore your physical dimension to its natural state of health, a state that is diminished through the stresses and struggles of daily use.

November 15

Laughter is medicine for the soul. Even if you don't feel like it, look in the mirror and laugh. You can't help but feel fantastic. William James said, "We don't laugh because we are happy. We are happy because we laugh." So start your day on a deliciously fun footing. Laugh, play and give thanks for all you have. Every day will be an exquisitely rewarding one if you choose it to be.

November 16

Writing things down is an incredibly important practice for self-discovery. The discipline of journaling transforms lives. Just as you get to know another person by having deep conversations with them, by journaling every morning you will come to know yourself through writing. Writing promotes clarity and clarity precedes mastery. And since your life is worth living, your life is definitely worth recording.

November 17

Most people use sleep as a drug. They use sleep to distract them and pass the time. As people begin to live a life that is incongruent with their biggest lives and their highest possibilities, a well of pain begins to form within them. Most people are not conscious of this—it happens at the subconscious level—but that does not mean it's not there, affecting them in every moment, in every choice and at every plane. So many among us use sleep to avoid that pain, to escape. But once you find your calling, you get excited. And the greater the excitement you will feel for this calling and for your life in general, the less you will need—or want—to sleep.

November 18

Designate some time every single day for personal renewal. Time spent recharging your batteries is never a waste but a necessary aspect of any peak performance routine. Recreation is about re-creation.

November 19

According to a study involving 17,000 Harvard alumni, it was found that every hour you exercise adds another three hours to your life. That's an excellent return on investment. As the sages say, The person who doesn't make time for exercise must eventually make time for illness.

November 20

While you cannot go on a major vacation every week, you certainly can go on a minor one. A mini-vacation begins with closing the door of your office, holding all calls and relaxing in your chair. Then close your eyes and begin taking deep breaths. Once you feel deeply at peace, begin to imagine you are at your favorite vacation spot. Vividly see the colors, hear the sounds and feel the emotions that this special place evokes. After only a few minutes of this mental escape, you will be rejuvenated, ready for the rest of the day ahead.

November 21

Music makes life better. Music can lift your mood, put the smile back on your face and add immeasurably to the quality of your life. Get serious about listening to music that inspires you. Build a collection of your favorite pieces and play something that fills your heart with joy every single day of the week. Listening to even a few minutes of music every day is a simple yet exceptionally powerful way to manage your moods and remain at your best.

November 22

The way you begin your day determines the way you will live your day. The first thirty minutes after you wake up are "The Platinum 30" since they are truly the most valuable moments of your day and have a profound influence on the quality of every minute that follows. If you have the wisdom and self-discipline to ensure that, during this key period, you think only the purest of thoughts and take only the greatest of actions, you will notice that your days will consistently unfold in the most marvelous ways.

November 23

Stress itself is not a bad thing. It can often help us perform at our best, expand beyond our limits and achieve things that would otherwise astonish us. The real problem lies in the fact that in this age of global anxiety we do not get enough relief from stress. So to revitalize yourself and nourish the deepest part of you, plan for a weekly period of peace—a weekly sabbatical—to get back to the simpler pleasures of life, pleasures that you may have given up as your days grew busier and your life more complex. Your weekly sabbatical does not have to last a full day. All you need are a few hours alone, perhaps on a quiet morning, when you can spend some time doing the things you love to do the most.

November 24

A simple technique to reshape your awareness involves nothing more than selecting a phrase, known as a mantra, that you will focus on at different times throughout the day. If it is inner peace and calm you seek, the phrase, known as a mantra, might be, "I am so grateful that I am a serene and tranquil person." If it is more confidence that you want, your mantra could be, "I am delighted that I am full of confidence and boundless courage." If it is material prosperity you are after, your saying might be, "I am so grateful that money and opportunity are flowing into my life." Repeat your mantras softly under your breath as you walk to work, as you wait in line or as you wash the dishes to fill otherwise unproductive times of your day with a powerful life improvement force. Try to say your personal phrase at least two hundred times a day for at least four weeks. The results will be profound as you take one giant step to finding the peace, prosperity and purpose your life requires. We become what we talk about.

November 25

Even more so than through laughter, we can connect with each other through the common sharing of our pain. If everyone in the world came together for half an hour and shared all of the personal suffering they have endured over the course of their lives, we would all be friends. There would be no enemies. There would be no wars.

November 26

One simple strategy to conquer the worry habit was to schedule specific times to worry—what I call "worry breaks." If we are facing a difficulty, it is easy to spend all our waking hours focusing on it. Instead, schedule fixed times to worry, say, thirty minutes every evening. During this worry session, you may wallow in your problems and brood over your difficulties. But after that period ends, train yourself to leave your troubles behind and do something more productive, such as going for a walk in natural surroundings or reading an inspirational book or having a heart-to-heart conversation with someone you admire or love. If during other times of the day you feel the need to worry, jot down what you want to worry about in a notebook, which you can then bring to your next worry break. This simple but powerful technique will help you gradually reduce the amount of time you spend worrying and eventually serve to eliminate this habit forever.

November 27

The gift of the knowledge age we live in is that you and I, and everyone around us, have the privilege to spend time, each and every day if we so choose, with the greatest thinkers who have walked on earth. We can befriend the world's most amazing people—whenever we want—through books, audio downloads and CDs, videos and other educational media. In spending time with history's wisest human beings, you cannot help but come away from the experience a fundamentally better person. Their stardust cannot help but rub off on you.

November 28

The more you can put a voice to your fear, the more the fear will move through you. The more you can talk about this, the more the hidden shadows come out into the light where they can be examined and released.

November 29

Begin to see your family as your own personal community and the place where most of your personal satisfaction will come from. Our greatest moments are the moments we spend with the people we love. Understand that through your family, you can gain a richer understanding of yourself and develop greater insight, knowledge and wisdom. Through your family, you can increase your humanity and actualize your inner strength. Leadership in your life begins with leadership in your home. Your family is your foundation, just like the launching pad of a rocket. Once it is secure and in perfect order, you can soar to heights previously unimagined.

November 30

The best way to inspire your children to develop into the kind of adults you dream of them becoming is to become the kind of adult you want them to be. All children believe that the way their parents act is the correct way to act. You teach them how to act by the way you act. Your values and beliefs become their values and beliefs. Your negative patterns will inevitably become their negative patterns. You need to remember that your children are always watching your every move.

December

Building Remarkable Relationships

Enjoy Life's Journey

December 1

After quality time, the second best gift you can give to your kids is the gift of a good example.

December 2

Speaking your truth means speaking from your heart. Far too many people in our world speak only in the words they know the people around them want to hear. They use their words to manipulate and control rather than to express their true feelings and build the kind of understanding that always leads to greater love. In using words that do not reflect what they really mean or how they truly feel, they live their lives in a state of spiritual dishonesty. Only by speaking your truth—what you truly feel, believe and know—will you be in a position to be the leader that you are destined to be. Speak your truth—even when your voice cracks.

December 3

Before anyone will lend you a hand, you must touch their heart. Be like the sun: the sun gives all it can give. But in return, all of the flowers, the trees and the plants grow toward it.

December 4

The little things are the big things. What small acts can you do today to deepen the bonds between you and the people you value the most? What random acts of kindness and senseless acts of beauty can you offer to someone in an effort to make his or her day just a little better? The irony of being more compassionate is that the very act of giving to others makes you feel better as well.

December 5

Too many people believe that listening involves nothing more than waiting for the other person to stop talking. And to make matters worse, while that person is speaking, we are all too often using that time to formulate our own response, rather than empathizing with the point being made. Taking the time to truly understand another's point of view shows that you value what he has to say and care about him as a person. When you start "getting behind the eyeballs" of the person who is speaking and try to see the world from his perspective, you will connect with him deeply and build high-trust relationships that last.

December 6

Focus on rebuilding your self-relationship. Get to know your deepest and truest values. Get to know your preferences and priorities—not those that others have taught you are the most important but those that you feel to be of the highest value. And remember that you can't give what you don't have. To love others you must first love yourself.

December 7

Forgiveness is a great act of spirit and personal courage. It is also one of the best ways to elevate the quality of your life. I have discovered that every minute you devote to thinking about someone who has wronged you is a minute you have stolen from a much worthier pursuit: connecting with those people who will elevate you.

December 8

Saying things we don't really mean becomes a habit when we practice it long enough. The real problem is that when you don't keep your word, you lose credibility. When you lose credibility, you break the bonds of trust. And breaking the bonds of trust ultimately leads to a string of broken relationships. Be a person of your word rather than being "all talk and no action." Say what you mean and mean what you say. That simple practice will have powerful results.

December 9

Talk is cheap and the evidence never lies. You can tell the world that your family comes first, but if you miss family dinners for business meetings most days of the week, the fact of the matter is that your family really does not come first. You can preach the power of reading and offer your children good books, but if you spend most of your free time watching sitcoms on TV, well then you really don't believe that learning is the priority you say it is.

December 10

Your primary duty as a parent is to become a builder of human trust. Trust forms the cornerstone of every great family culture.

December 11

Cultivating great friendships is one of the surest ways to find more happiness and joy in your life. Recent studies show that those with a wide circle of friends and family live longer, laugh more and worry less. But friendships, like all other good things in life, take time, energy and commitment. To build deeper friendships, you must be willing to move out of your comfort zone, break the ice with people you might not know very well and show sincere warmth. If you plant the seeds of friendship, you are bound to receive a rich harvest of great friends.

December 12

Although being a parent is a great joy, it is also a privilege that involves tremendous responsibility. We need to develop the skills of excellent parents. We cannot just hope that the way we are raising our kids is the right way and pray that we will be lucky enough that they become thoughtful, caring and wise adults. Take the initiative to improve your parenting abilities by attending seminars, reading books and listening to audio downloads and CDs by the leading thinkers in this field. Then have the courage to keep trying to refine the ideas learned in the laboratory of your own life in order to find the parenting strategies that best suit your family. Those miraculous years of your sons' and daughters' childhoods will never come again. So act now.

December 13

We are all connected at an invisible level. We are all brothers and sisters who belong to the same family. It's only an illusion that we are separate. Sages have told us that for thousands of years—we are all cut from the same cloth, and when you hurt another person, you hurt yourself as well. Be the kindest person you know.

December 14

It is easy to fall into the habit of condemning others, even those we love most. We criticize the way someone eats or the manner in which she speaks. We focus on the most minute details and find fault with the smallest of issues. But what we focus on grows. And if we keep focusing on a small weakness in someone, it will continue to grow in our minds until we perceive it to be a big problem in that person. To live a happier, more peaceful life, begin to see that the richness of our society comes from its diversity. What makes relationships, communities and countries great are not the things that we have in common but the differences that make us unique. Rather than looking for things to criticize in those around you, why not begin to respect the differences?

December 15

There is something special about being in the presence of a person who is genuinely humble. Practicing humility shows that you respect others and reminds us that there is so much for us yet to learn. It sends a signal to those around you that you are open to receiving the gift of their knowledge and listening to what they have to say. The more you are as a person, the less you need to prove yourself to others.

December 16

It's been said that laughter is the shortest distance between human hearts. When we laugh together, all the social constructs that keep us apart fall to the wayside and we connect as real people. It's a beautiful thing to behold.

December 17

When you blame others for the things that anger or irritate you, you lose a precious chance to get to know more of the shadows that are controlling you. You lose the opportunity to go deep and bring what was within the realm of the subconscious into the realm of the conscious, where it can be healed and released. Blaming others is excusing yourself.

December 18

Realize that the most noble thing you can do is to give to others. The sages of the East call it the process of "shedding the shackles of self." It is all about losing your self-consciousness and starting to focus on a higher purpose. This might be in the form of giving more to those around you, whether this means your time or your energy: these truly are your two most valuable resources.

December 19

Compassion and daily acts of kindness make life far richer. Take the time to meditate every morning on the good you will do for others during your day. The sincere words of praise to those who least expect it, the gestures of warmth offered to friends in need, the small tokens of affection to members of your family for no reason at all, all add up to a much more wonderful way to live.

December 20

Live your children's childhood. Few things are as meaningful as being a part of your children's childhood. What is the point of climbing the steps of success if you have missed the first steps of your own kids?

December 21

It's a strange world we live in. We can send a message across the world with pinpoint accuracy, yet we have trouble walking across the street to meet a new neighbor. We spend more time watching television than we do connecting with our children. We say we want to change the world but are not willing to change ourselves. Then, as the sun sets on our lives and we allow ourselves some time for a little deep reflection, we catch a glimpse of the joys we could have experienced, the kindnesses we could have given, and the people we could have been. But by then, it's too late.

December 22

Love is what we need more of in this world. And I'm not only referring to loving other people. We must show love to our work. We must show love to our surroundings, and most importantly, we must show love to ourselves. Only then can we really give our love fully to other people. Everything you do as you live out your days should speak of love.

December 23

When you have not forgiven someone, it is almost as if you are carrying that person on your back—which is a very heavy load. And once you forgive them, you release them. You can finally move on with life. They are no longer pulling you down. You become much more free as a human being.

December 24

Forgiving someone is different from condoning his or her behavior. Forgiving them is simply seeing that people in pain do painful things. I encourage you to understand that people who hurt other people have themselves been hurt. People who do not love themselves cannot show love to others. And people who do not have any self-respect have no idea how to give respect to others.

December 25

Do you know how happy every person on the planet would feel if they made a little bit of time every day to be of greater service to others? Please think about the joy that enters a person's being when they dedicate themselves to creating real and lasting value for other people? Helping other people get to their dreams is, when viewed from this frame of reference, a great gift you give yourself. But too many people don't see this truth.

Enjoy Life's Journey

December 26

Start to revere life again and celebrate all its wonders. Awaken yourself to the power you have to make things happen. Once you do, Life will brilliantly help you to work wonders.

Enjoy Life's Journey

December 27

Do what you need to do to develop a love for life. Make the time to get excited about the simple pleasures of life, the ones we cherished as children. Most of us don't appreciate what we have until we lose it.

Enjoy Life's Journey

December 28

Life is such a fragile thing. It is a priceless treasure that we are given to guard and make use of to the best of our ability. That it will not come again is what makes it so sacred.

December 29

Really commit to becoming a person who lives life in a constant state of gratitude and positive expectation. Dream big dreams, but also savor the place where you find yourself to be at any time. The road really is as good as the end. When you can maintain this frame of mind, life will be sure to shower its abundance on you.

December 30

Life's a game. Don't take it too seriously. Have fun. Dance. Laugh. Love. And maintain a rich amount of perspective.

Enjoy Life's Journey

December 31

Have fun while you are advancing along the path of your goals, purpose and dreams. Never forget the importance of living with unbridled exhilaration. Never neglect to see the exquisite beauty in all living things. Today and this very moment that you and I are sharing is a gift. Remain spirited, joyful and curious. Stay focused on your lifework and on giving selfless service to others. Yet have a great time along the way because your life is a treasure to be celebrated.

ABOUT THE AUTHOR

Robin Sharma is one of the world's top experts on leadership and personal success. The author of eight major international bestsellers, including *The Greatness Guide* and *Who Will Cry When You Die?*, Robin is the CEO of Sharma Leadership International Inc., a boutique training firm with a simple mission: to help people and organizations get to world class. Clients include Microsoft, Nike, FedEx, BP, IBM and GE. His enormously popular website, **robinsharma.com**, offers his blog, podcasts and robinsharmaTV, as well as information on booking him for a presentation to your group.